CH/Min

KIDSTORIES

Seasonal and Topical Sermons for Children

Betsy Larson

BAKER BOOK HOUSE
Grand Rapids, Michigan 49506

ISBN: 0-8010-5598-9

Second printing, September 1982

CONTENTS

1. The Bionic Man and Woman 7
2. The Tapestry 9
3. Scott's Sunflower and Eddie's Pumpkin 11
4. Yellow Ribbon Song 13
5. Does God Have a Lap? 15
6. Spaghetti 17
7. Rotating Restaurant 19
8. Messy Rooms 22
9. Silver Dollars and Magnets 24
10. Vertical and Horizontal 26
11. Authority on Strike 27
12. Enjoy Now 30
13. Skateboards 33
14. Bow and Arrow 36
15. Warm Fuzzies and Cold Pricklies 37
16. Toys and No Toys 39
17. Crutches 41
18. Seeing Through a Glass Darkly 43
19. The Smashed Paper Cup 45
20. The Escalators 48
21. Lost in the Supermarket 51
22. Three Hugs a Day 53

23. The Stump that Sprouted 55
24. Thanksgiving Bubblegum 57
25. The Birds and the Blizzard (Christmas) 59
26. Blackout at Tom's House 61
27. Traffic Signs 63
28. Celebrating Women 65
29. Jimmy's Cozy Bed 68
30. Anne and Kathy 70
31. The Simple Life 72
32. Invisible Friends 75
33. Two Sticks in the Stream 77
34. Nursery Room Window 80
35. Job's Footprints 82
36. Strawberry Easter 85
37. Pit Stops (Memorial Day) 88
38. Butterfly (Spring) 90
39. God and Vacations (Summer) 93
40. New Boy at School (Autumn) 95
Subject Index 98

1

THE BIONIC MAN AND WOMAN

How many of you know about the Six-Million-Dollar Man and the Bionic Woman? What makes them different than regular people?

That's right. They both have special power in their legs and right arms, and Steve has extra power in his eyes while Jaime has super-sensitive ears. They can lift heavy things and they can jump high (eyes scan the ceiling). No matter how hard an ordinary person tried, he could never jump as high as Jaime or Steve, could he?

Did you know that each one of you has a special power, too? Your special power is called love-power, and it is planted inside you, just like Steve's bionics are planted in him. Only your love-power doesn't come from a little machine that can break down or stop working. It comes from God and it never breaks down.

Some of you probably didn't even know you had a special power. Do you know how you can make it work?

The next time you are in trouble—let's say you have a fight or you are angry with someone—then try plugging your power in. You do this by saying, "Help, God! I'm in trouble. Please send me some love-power." You can do this silently or you can say it out loud but you have to really do it. Plug your power in.

After you have plugged in, expect your love-power to work. After all, when Steve goes to kick down a door, he doesn't stop and say, "Oh, dear, I wonder if my bionic leg is working. Maybe it won't work. I'd better not try." No, he doesn't do that; he gives a big kick and *expects* his bionic leg to work! In the same way, when you say, "Help, God! I'm in trouble. Send me some love-power," you expect it to come. Watch it start working. All the angriness will drain away and love will flow. It can turn you from fighting to making peace and being friends.

Grownups call this love-power "the grace of God" and it works even better than knocking your enemy down, like Steve might do, or jumping up over them, like Jaime might do. In fact, your own special power is the strongest force in the *world*. Did you know that? It is even stronger than bionics. Try it and you will see what I mean. Love-power really works.

2

THE TAPESTRY

(Speaker holds up a large piece of needlework, with the back side facing the children.) Who can tell me what this is?

You can't see any clear picture, can you? All you can see is a bunch of knots and threads that cross over, and even the colors are mixed-up. Sometimes our lives seem like that. We have a bad day, and we feel like one of these knots. Or, we get all mixed-up and feel like these tangled threads. We think that life is a mess and it looks like the back of this tapestry to us: certainly not beautiful, but all full of knots and tangles.

But there *is* beauty to life. God has a beautiful plan for everything, even a special plan for *your* life! He knows exactly what it is and it is a lovely picture—like this (speaker shows the front of the tapestry).

See, this looks wonderful, doesn't it? And yet, this (shows back of tapestry) is the way we sometimes see our lives.

How can we see things the way God sees them? How can we think more like God thinks?

1. When we pray, we talk to God. We get to know Him; we get closer to Him.

2. The Bible tells us the story of God. If we learn all about it, then we understand more of how God thinks. We understand more how God sees the world.

3. And of course, when we die, we go to be with God. And then we see everything like He does.

So, let's remember this (speaker holds up the back side of the tapestry). This is the way *we* see the world, and (reverse tapestry) this is the way *God* sees the world. Let's try to get closer to God so we can see the world this way, too.

Prayer: Father, we are learning that you have a plan, even a beautiful plan for our life. Help us draw closer to you, so we can see it, too. Amen.

3

SCOTT'S SUNFLOWER AND EDDIE'S PUMPKIN

I have a friend named Eddie. He has a garden behind his house. His friend Scott has a garden, too. In Scott's garden is a sunflower. Have any of you ever seen a big sunflower? Have you ever grown one in your family's garden?

Scott's sunflower was a beauty. It was big and tall and sturdy, and every day Scott and Eddie checked it out when they were playing. It grew way over their heads, so they had to look up to see the huge round yellow flower on top.

Eddie really admired Scott's sunflower. He wished he had one as big as Eddie's. So, the next spring, Eddie planted a seed. Only, you know what? He didn't plant a sunflower seed; he planted a seed that was almost the same size as a sunflower seed but it was a pumpkin seed.

You know what happened, don't you? The seed began to grow, and Eddie got all excited when the green leaves poked out. He watered it, kept the weeds out of the way, and made sure it had lots of sunlight.

One day, though, he noticed it wasn't growing like a sunflower should. Instead of growing up straight and tall, it was creeping along the ground. What kind of a sunflower creeps along the ground?

So Eddie tried to fix it. He tied up the green vine and leaves to the fence by the garden, hoping it would grow up straight. But it didn't. It kept drooping down, running this way and that way all over the fence.

Eddie was really mad. This wasn't what he intended at all. Even though his friends admired his healthy pumpkin plant and the big orange pumpkin growing on it, Eddie wanted a sunflower—big and strong, taller than he was, with a big flower full of sunflower seeds.

God has a seed He wants us to plant, too. It is the seed of loving each other.

Sometimes we plant different seeds, thinking they will be just as good. We work very hard, we get all our jobs done, or we raise a lot of money and give it to the church, or we study very hard and learn everything we can. All these things are good things to do, and God admires all these seeds. But the *special* seed God wants us to plant is loving each other. And if we plant every other seed except this one, all is not right. We become very smart or very rich or very hard workers, but we don't have that special flower—love for each other.

Pumpkins are good. Corn is good. Beans are good. But let's remember to plant that one most important seed in our lives—loving each other.

4

YELLOW RIBBON SONG

I want to see if you can guess the name of a song. I'll give you a clue, first (holds up yellow ribbon). What is this? Right, a yellow ribbon! Now who can tell me the name of this song? (Pianist or organist plays "Tie a Yellow Ribbon Round the Old Oak Tree.")

That's right. The song is "Tie a Yellow Ribbon Round the Old Oak Tree." Have any of you heard it before, on the radio, maybe? It's a good foot-tapping song and it tells an interesting story. The song starts:

> Tie a yellow ribbon round the old oak tree.
> It's been three long years.
> Do you still love me?*

A person just like us is saying this as he rides a bus back home. Do you know where he's been? He's been in jail, because he did something wrong. He had to stay in prison for three long years, but now he has paid for the thing he did wrong and he is heading back home.

As he rides along in the bus, jostling and bouncing around, he is wondering, *Does my special someone at home still love me?*

Have you ever done something bad, and then worried that someone wouldn't love you any more?

*Lyrics used by permission of Levine & Brown Music, New York.

Let's see what happened to this person on the bus. He wrote a letter when he was in prison, telling his special someone to tie a yellow ribbon around a certain tree if she still loved him. He knew the bus would be driving right past that tree (it was right next to the road), and so he could tell, if the tree had no ribbon, that she didn't love him any more. Then he could stay on the bus and keep riding and go away forever.

He didn't want to go away forever. He wanted to come back home and be loved. But he wasn't sure she would welcome him back.

So, as they got closer and closer to home, he looked out the bus window (peering gesture). Finally he could hardly stand to look any longer, so he told the person next to him about the yellow ribbon and had him look for it, instead. That person told the rest of the people on the bus, and they all looked for the yellow ribbon. And as the song comes to an end, it says:

> . . . the whole bus is cheering
> and I can't believe I see
> a hundred yellow ribbons
> round the old oak tree.

Well, what do you think those yellow ribbons meant? Yes, she loved him! And loved him and loved him and loved him and loved him—a hundred times more than he had expected! How do you think those one hundred yellow ribbons made him feel when he saw them all? Yes, it's like a man named C. S. Lewis said: he was "Surprised by joy."

God is like that. When we have done something wrong, we feel bad. And if we come to God and say we are sorry and will try to make it right and not do it any more, *then* we feel like asking: "Do you still love me?" And God's answer is yes, a hundred times yes! Just like the hundred yellow ribbons He surprises us by joy!

5

DOES GOD HAVE A LAP?

I want to talk today about nightmares. How many of you have awakened in the middle of the night afraid because of scary things you were dreaming about?

Everybody has nightmares at some time or other. People seem to have them more often when they are young, like you, though. I know a boy named Rick that sometimes had bad dreams. He would call his mother and she would come and sit on the side of his bed and hug him and talk to him. Pretty soon he'd feel better and fall back asleep.

One time when she came, she suggested that Rick ask God to help him when he was afraid because of a bad dream. Rick thought about it, but then he patted his mother's arm and said, "I need someone right now with skin on!"

His mother smiled and said she was glad she could help him feel better. Then she said maybe both of them could ask God to help Rick with his bad dreams.

God loves you. He doesn't want you to feel that awful afraid feeling, alone in the night. That feeling doesn't come from Him. A famous psalm in the Bible says:

"Yea, though I walk through the valley of the shadow of death, I will fear no evil: for thou art with me; thy rod and thy staff they comfort me" (Ps. 23:4, KJV).

If we used words that we use today, we would say the same thing this way: "Even when I walk through the dark valley of death, I will not be afraid, for you (God) are close beside me, guarding me, and taking care of me all the way."

Well, that sounds good, doesn't it? You see, even the people who wrote the Bible knew what nightmares were and they knew God helps us when we are afraid. He stays right by us and comforts us.

"He comforts us?" Rick asked his mother.

"Sure He does, Rick." she said.

"Does God have a lap?" Rick asked her.

His mother smiled again. "Think about the happiest, most loving time you can ever remember. Maybe it was when we were by the fireplace and it was snowing out and we were all cozy indoors, or maybe when we fell asleep in the hammock. Remember that?"

"Or when we got the new puppy and he curled up in my lap . . . ," Rick remembered.

"Okay, are you remembering that time?" his mother asked. "That's how it feels when God comforts you."

"Wow! Really?" Rick said. "God must have the biggest, coziest lap in the world!"

Yes, I guess you could say God does. And each one of us needs to crawl into God's lap and be comforted sometimes. Rick and his mother prayed together that his bad dreams wouldn't come back that night, and they didn't.

This is an idea for you: if you are having bad dreams, pray with someone else, or even by yourself, that God will protect you. You can even pray this before you fall asleep at night.

God does have a nice, big comforting lap.

6

SPAGHETTI

Who knows how to cook something? What can you cook?

I remember when I first learned how to cook spaghetti. You boil those long white noodles in a pot of water for a while and then you eat them with spaghetti sauce over them. Anyway, I had the spaghetti in the pot and the water began to boil. It bubbled up and popped and bubbled up again. Have any of you ever seen water boiling in a pot?

So there I was watching the water boil when the phone rang. I answered it, but it was for my mother, so I had to run all over to find her. By the time we both came back to the kitchen phone, something smelled funny. Can you guess what had happened?

Right. The spaghetti pot had boiled over. It made a sticky mess all over the top of the stove. I had to clean it up, but when my mom was done on the phone, she told me a cooking trick: whenever you are boiling something in a pot and you don't want it to boil over, put some oil in the water, like salad oil. So, I got some fresh water and some more spaghetti and started over. The water began to roll around and boil. Then Mom poured about a spoonful of salad oil on the boiling water. It kept right on bubbling and boiling but it didn't rise up the side of the pot and boil over. It just stayed right where it was and boiled along. I watched it for a long time.

My mom said that cooking trick comes from the Bible. It's called pouring oil on troubled waters—waters that are about to boil over and make a mess.

As God's people we are supposed to be the helpers that keep the world's trouble from boiling over, just like that little spoonful of oil in my spaghetti pot.

How can we do that? We must ask God to help us, and His love will come to us and keep the world from boiling over.

Prayer: Dear Father, thank you for your amazing grace that keeps love flowing in the world and keeps the world from boiling over. Please fill us with your love. Amen.

7

ROTATING RESTAURANT

I know a boy who got to go to a fancy restaurant with his mom and dad and baby brother. Have any of you ever gone to a fancy restaurant?

This was a special restaurant. It was on top of a tall building and the restaurant went around while you ate your dinner. You could sit right at your table, and out the windows, see the city going by! It was really something!

"Now son," Billy's dad said, "to get to this revolving restaurant, we ride up the side of the building in a glass elevator. It ought to be quite a sight."

"Wow! A glass elevator!" Billy said.

When the elevator whooshed up, Billy felt like he was flying. He looked at all the city around him getting smaller and smaller. Soon the buildings looked like little blocks and the streets were stripes along the blocks.

"We're here!" his mother said.

"I get to sit next to the window!" Billy shouted.

This was a very proper restaurant. Guests had to be polite. All the visitors there were dressed up and they spoke softly.

"Billy," his mother whispered, "there's no place to put the baby down except by you. Will you watch him if I put his infant seat down on the floor next to you?"

"Yeah, okay," said Billy. "Look at how far down the cars are, Mom. The people look like ants."

"Yes, and there's your dad's blue building—see Billy?—over by the bank tower."

Billy could hardly keep his eyes off the windows, as their table slowly moved around. All during dinner he watched. "Look, Dad, a thundercloud over there. I wonder if we will see lightning come out of it?" Billy saw airplanes and flocks of birds going by. He saw a long moving snake-like thing that turned out to be a train, chugging along.

Just as he was finishing his french fries, he heard a lot of noise from the other side of the restaurant. "How's the baby, Billy? He certainly has been quiet," his mother said. Billy looked down and the baby *wasn't there.*

"What do you *mean* he isn't there?" his father said.

His mother jumped up and looked: "He's gone! My baby—where is he?"

Billy was scared. How could he have lost the baby? That was his *only* baby brother.

His father threw his napkin down on the table. His mother ran to the waitress, talking to her, sounding worried. But the waitress just smiled and patted Mother's arm. Then she took Billy's mom and dad around the restaurant to the other side, and there in the middle of all the noise was Billy's baby brother. He was sitting in his infant seat, waving his arms and laughing, while people leaned over their dinner tables to him and said, "Kitchy, kitchy coo. . . ."

"How did he get way over here?" Billy asked.

"He didn't go anywhere," the waitress explained. "He stayed right there on the same place on the floor—but your table was slowly moving around in a circle. You moved away from him and didn't even notice."

"Oh!" his father laughed. "And then all these other people's tables moved up to the baby and passed on, table by table?"

"Yes," said the waitress. "We wondered whose baby it was, but he was having so much fun we hated to bother him."

Billy's mother scooped up the baby. "Well, at least he's all right," she smiled. "Next time, Billy, when I ask you to watch the baby, do it."

"Yes, Mom," Billy said, feeling bad.

"Well, it's pretty hard to watch a baby and see out the windows, too," his father said. "Let's put the baby up on the table and then we can all look outside and he won't go anywhere." So that's what they did.

Billy always remembered the awful feeling he had when he was supposed to do something and didn't do it. So he tried harder to do a good job at whatever he had to do. "The case of the missing baby" helped him remember.

8

MESSY ROOMS

How many of you don't like to keep your room neat and clean? Well, you are like most people. It takes time to pick up all our stuff, and most of us would rather do something else more fun.

I know a boy named Melvin who had the messiest room you could ever see. It was so bad his mother wouldn't even go into it. There was some food under the bed that had gone moldy and smelled funny, the ants had found an old bag of Oreoes in the closet, and Melvin's dirty clothes were piled all over the floor. He couldn't see any part of the floor at all—only dirty clothes. If you wanted to go in Melvin's room (and almost nobody did) you had to know which clothes to step on, because under some of them were Lego blocks, roller skates, and slippery comic books.

Melvin and his mother argued about his room all the time. When she couldn't stand it any longer and the ants were starting to get in other rooms in the house, Melvin's mother would wade in and clean it up. Melvin came home and thought he was in the wrong house.

Messy Melvin went on for years like this. Finally, the family solved the problem. An old trailer no one used anymore was parked in the back yard. Melvin asked if he could move into that trailer, using it as his room. After talking about it, the whole family agreed. So Melvin moved out to the trailer.

Everyone was happy: Melvin's mother painted his old room with fresh bright paint and set up her sewing machine in there. Melvin could be as messy as he wanted, and no one bothered him in the trailer.

After a while, though, Melvin's little brother said, "You smell funny." His sister said, "Melvin needs a bath." A bath? There was no bathtub or shower in the trailer. So Melvin forgot about it. He began noticing that kids moved away from him on the school bus. All his friends were too busy to play with him. He was even getting kind of lonesome by himself in the trailer. He missed his family.

One day he lost a book. He was just at the most exciting part, and now he couldn't find the book! He hunted all over the trailer, through the piles of clothes on the floor, through all the junk under his bed. While he was looking he found some allowance money and a new magazine he hadn't even seen yet. Finally he stood up and looked around the trailer. It looked like it had been stirred with a stick. And he still hadn't found his book.

"This is dumb," he decided. "I can't find things, kids say I smell funny, it's getting lonely out here. Other people can keep their rooms neat; I ought to be able to, too."

So without telling anyone, Melvin began to clean up. He didn't like to spend all Saturday doing it, so he quickly straightened the trailer up each morning before school. It began to be a game with him, to see if anyone would notice.

People noticed, all right. And as winter came on and the trailer got too cold, Melvin moved back into the house. But his family didn't mind. Now he was nice to live with because he had learned for himself that cleanliness is better than messiness.

Melvin also learned that God's way is an orderly way. So now Melvin takes that few extra minutes every day to straighten up. He even helps his mother clean the rest of the house. The house is more peaceful and the whole family is happier.

9

SILVER DOLLARS AND MAGNETS

I have a birthday story for you this morning. My friend Billy was happy because it was his birthday, and his Grandpa had given him a silver dollar. It was big and silvery (pass one around)—bigger than any coin he had ever seen. See how big it is? Bigger than a dime or a nickel or even a quarter. Billy was really proud of it and ran outside to show it to his friends.

They all wanted to see it and feel it and hold it. Pretty soon they got to pushing and shoving, saying "It's my turn!" and then the silver dollar dropped to the street and began to roll. It rolled along the edge of the street and rolled and rolled . . . until, *"Plunk!"* it dropped into the storm gutter!

"Oh, no!" yelled Billy. All his friends leaned over the square holes in the gutter and looked down, way down into the hole. There was the silver dollar at the bottom, shining away.

The hole was too deep for Billy to reach bottom with his arm. So he ran back to his house and took a magnet off the refrigerator (hold up a horseshoe-shaped magnet). Billy knew that magnets stuck to shiny metal, so he tied a string around the magnet and slowly lowered it down the gutter hole.

"That isn't gonna work, Billy," one of the older kids said.

"Why not?" said Billy.

"Because silver dollars don't stick to magnets. No coins stick to magnets."

"They don't? Why not? They're metal and they're shiny."

"I dunno. Coins just aren't attracted to magnets. They don't stick to 'em." (Demonstrate how the magnet and silver dollar don't attract each other.) Sure enough, no matter how close Billy got the magnet, it wouldn't stick to the silver dollar so he could pull it up out of the gutter.

Later Billy thought about how God sort of fishes from heaven and tries to find people who will "stick" with Him—who are attracted to Him. Some people are not attracted to Him—like the silver dollar rejected the magnet—and some people are. *What makes the difference?* Billy wondered. Some people say "Leave me alone, God. I don't want anything to do with you." And some people say, "Okay, God: here I am. I want to get to know you and be your friend."

People who are willing "stick" to God when He fishes for them. All you have to do is say yes to God inside yourself, and then God begins to be your friend and your whole life gets better and better.

By the way, Billy did finally get his silver dollar back. Do you know how he did it? He put bubblegum on the end of a long pole and poked it down, and the silver dollar stuck to the bubblegum. Anything sticks to bubblegum.

Prayer: Dear God, we want to be your friends. Right now, while you are calling us, we want to say yes to you. Yes, God, come be with us, now and forever. Amen.

10

VERTICAL AND HORIZONTAL

Who knows what this is? (Hold up two sticks in a "cross" formation.) Right, this is a cross. There is one on the altar, and there is one on this Bible, and sometimes people wear crosses on chains around their necks. Why do we have all these crosses around?

Right, to remember Jesus. He died on a cross for you and for me. So this cross helps us remember Jesus and the gospel story.

You will notice each cross has an up-and-down part (hold longer stick up), which is called the vertical, and a sideways part (hold up shorter stick), which is called the horizontal.

This (hold longer stick between your eyes and the ceiling) helps me remember that we are to love God and learn about Him—God and me, up and down, vertical.

This (hold shorter stick between yourself and the child next to you) helps me remember we are to love and help other people— you and me, side by side, horizontal love.

God wants us to love Him—vertical—and to love others—horizontal. Jesus explained this by saying, "You shall love the Lord your God with all your heart and all your soul and all your mind (hold up vertical) and your neighbor as yourself" (hold up horizontal).

So, the next time you see a plain cross, you might think about that. God wants us to learn to love Him because He is so wonderful, and to love other people because He loves them, too.

11

AUTHORITY ON STRIKE

Who gave the Ten Commandments? God did. Why should people have to do what God says? Because God is wisest and strongest and in charge of the world. He's the boss.

Are your mothers and fathers supposed to obey God's rules? Sure, God is their authority, like their boss. They are supposed to do what He says. How about you—do you have a boss at home? Who? Your mom or dad is your boss at home. God has made it so that you are to do what they say. Sometimes it is hard, isn't it? But it helps to remember that that is God's plan: you are to obey your mom and dad. This plan works out well if everyone does his part; if your parents obey God and you obey your parents, everything is fine.

But I know one little boy who wouldn't obey. His name was Chuck. He decided he was tired of doing what his mother said. Why should he have to carry out the trash and clean his room and do all the things she told him? What was he, a slave? So one night he said, "I quit! I'm not going to do what you tell me anymore." His parents just stared at him, and then he went outside to play. He stayed out long past his bedtime.

The next morning he slept too long and came rushing into the kitchen. "Quick, where's breakfast, Mom? I'm late for school!"

His mother was stretched out on the couch reading a magazine.

"I'm on strike," his mother said. "I don't make breakfast around here anymore."

Hoo boy! Poor Chuck rushed around the kitchen and got an apple and a stale cookie for breakfast. Then he saw his father wander into the kitchen still wearing pajamas. "What are you doing home today, Dad? It's a work day."

"Oh, I'm on strike," his father said. "I decided I'm not going to work all day just to bring home money for this family." Chuck was really surprised. His father always went to work. What was going on here, he wondered.

"Dad, can I have some lunch money? I'm in a rush because I'm late for school."

(Speaker holds up hand.) "Nope, Chuck. I am going to spend all my money on myself. Today I'm going to go out and buy a bowling ball."

His father was sure acting funny, Chuck thought. But he didn't have time to worry about it. He ran to ask his mother for lunch money, calling, "Hey, Mom, can I . . ."

(Speaker holds up hand.) "Nope, Chuck. I'm on strike. I don't give out lunch money anymore."

"But what will I do for lunch?" Chuck said. His mother just went back to reading her magazine.

Boy, this was awful.

Chuck went up to his piggy bank and by the time he got enough money out for his lunch, he heard the school bus go by his house. Oh, dear. "Mom," he said. "I missed the bus. Will you drive me to school, please?"

His mother said, "Nope. I'm on strike. I don't drive children to school anymore." So Chuck had to walk all the way to school.

That night Chuck's mom cooked no dinner, and his dad was nowhere around. Chuck was getting pretty sick of this whole idea of being on strike. If he quit doing what he was supposed to, as a little boy—that was one thing. But if everyone else quit doing what they were supposed to—that was awful!

How could Chuck get his mom and dad back to doing their

regular things, like cooking meals and mowing lawns and going to work and sharing? Maybe he should do his part.

So that night Chuck went out to the kitchen and by himself, without being told, carried out the trash. His mom was sure happy to see that. She and Chuck and his dad had a good talk about working together, everyone doing his part. It turned out that Chuck's mom and dad didn't like being on strike, either. They loved Chuck and wanted their family to work right.

Now Chuck knows he is to respect and obey his parents, and his parents are to respect and obey God.

12

ENJOY NOW

I know a boy about your age, and he has a new baby in his neighborhood. Are there any new babies in your neighborhood?

Billy had known this new baby was coming for a long time because Mrs. Crump across the street had been complaining for months. (Whining voice) "Oh, I will be so glad when this baby is finally here!" she'd say. "I wonder if this baby is ever going to come."

The baby finally did come, but Billy didn't get to see it. It was too little, Mrs. Crump said, and she was too tired to have company. "I will certainly be glad when this baby begins to sleep through the night, so I can get some rest," she'd say.

One day Billy was riding his Big Wheel on the sidewalk with his mom walking beside him when he saw a mailbox with a huge pink bow on it. "What's that for?" he asked. "And look, Mom, there's an even bigger pink bow across their garage door."

His mom smiled. "I think that's there to tell the world that this house has a new baby, a little girl. Pink for a girl, blue for a boy." Billy looked at the house and there by the front door was a lady in a lawn chair with a buggy next to her. "Let's go up and see the baby," his mother said.

Billy and his mom met the lady. She was nice. Her name was Delight Johnson. "Would you like to see the baby?" she asked Billy.

He was surprised at how small it was. "Look, Billy, how little and how perfect her fingernails are."

"And look at that little mouth," said his mother behind him. "Doesn't it look like a rosebud?"

"Why is she waving her hands around like that?" Billy asked.

"She's watching them move. She thinks that's interesting. And maybe she is trying to figure out how she can get the hand closer to her or get her thumb in her mouth."

"Can't she do that?" Billy asked Mrs. Johnson.

"Not yet. But babies are amazing things. She can already see and smile, and I bet by the time you come next, she'll have figured how to make her hand move the way she wants it to."

"Yeah?" said Billy, staring at the baby.

Billy watched the Johnson baby grow and change. Every time he rode his bike up the driveway, the baby could do something new. Soon she could laugh, and then sit up. Then she learned to say "Da-da" and then "Bee-wee" for Billy.

But all Billy ever heard about Mrs. Crump's baby was how many diapers he used up and how tired he made Mrs. Crump. She said she wished he would get out of diapers soon.

Mrs. Johnson's baby girl, Violet, grew so she could walk. So did Mrs. Crump's baby, George. Mrs. Johnson said, "Look at how sturdy her little legs are. Isn't it wonderful she's walking?"

Mrs. Crump said, "I will be so glad when that baby is out of this toddler stage. He gets into everything. What a mess!"

Billy watched Violet and George grow up until they both started their first day of school. "Isn't that something—she's going off to school!" Mrs. Johnson said. "She's learning so much. She already knows her alphabet."

Mrs. Crump said, "George is only going to kindergarten. I will be so glad when he's gone all day to school, then I can get some work done around here."

This went on until both Violet and George went to college. Mrs. Johnson said, "Imagine Violet going to college, learning all those new things. She's getting ready to be a teacher. Isn't that wonderful?"

Mrs. Crump said, "I wish George was through college. It costs so much money!"

After Violet went away to college Mrs. Johnson learned how to be a librarian. Every day she was in the children's room at the library, helping kids find good books and laughing and reading to them during story hour. Mrs. Crump stayed home and complained with George away at college. He never came home to visit her, she said. He was a bad son, and she didn't see why he wouldn't come home.

I see why he wouldn't come home, don't you?

The last time Billy saw Mrs. Johnson she was having a birthday party for Violet's little girl. Billy had seen Mrs. Johnson's birthday parties before; they looked like a lot of fun. Billy thought about Mrs. Johnson. Why was she always so happy? She seemed to enjoy whatever she was doing.

Mrs. Crump wasn't happy because she was always wishing things were different. She didn't try to see what's good about right now. Billy decided it would be nicer to live like Delight Johnson—enjoying now. So he tried it and it worked for him.

Let's try it. What's nice about right now? We're in church, it's comfortable and quiet, our family is here, God loves us, we don't have any work we have to do, there isn't a war on, it's a nice day outside. . . .

Enjoy right now. God gave us life, and He wants us to enjoy it.

Prayer: Thank you, God, for the gift of life. Help us to learn to enjoy it, right now. Amen.

13

SKATEBOARDS

Does anyone here know what a skateboard is? (Borrow one to show, if possible.) Have you seen kids riding these skateboards on driveways and down hills?

I know a boy—we'll call him Rick—who was six years old and he wanted a skateboard. He saw older kids riding them down the hill in front of his house and they went, "Whoosh!" they went by so fast. They could curve around the road and do turns and they even had things tied on their legs that would flutter in the wind when they went by. It sure looked like fun. Rick sat on his front porch and wished he had a skateboard, too.

"No," said his mother. "You are only six. That's too young. Besides, skateboards are dangerous."

So Rick sat on his porch some more, sighing (heavy sigh), wishing he had a skateboard.

He asked his father, but his father was reading the newspaper. (Gruff voice) "Go ask your mother," he said.

"But I already did," Rick said.

"Hmmmm . . . ," Father said.

Poor Rick. Nobody seemed to understand how much he wanted a skateboard. But then Rick remembered something he heard right here in church: God always listens; God always understands. Rick had an idea: he would ask God for a skateboard!

That night he prayed. He got down on his knees and said, "Please, God, may I have a skateboard? Nobody else listens or will let me have one, so I'm asking you. Thank you, God, and goodnight. Amen."

Nothing happened the next day, although Rick was watching and waiting for God to answer his prayer. The next day, Saturday, Rick woke up hearing all kinds of hammering and sawing going on under his bedroom window. He went to see what the noise was. The big teenage boys next door were building something out of wood in their driveway.

"Whatcha building?" Rick asked Tommy.

"Hi, Rick. We're building a ramp for our skateboards."

"A ramp?" said Rick. "What's that?"

"See that garage roof up there?" Tommy said. "We begin riding our skateboards up on the roof, ride down the ramp, way down here, then up again on this hill part, and then down to the driveway. It's gonna be neat."

Rick looked all the way up to the garage roof. "Boy, that looks awfully high," he said. "What if you fall off?"

"Ah, I won't fall off. I'm good on a skateboard," Tommy said.

Rick got busy with other things and forgot about it until he heard a siren and then saw an ambulance in Tommy's driveway. What do you think had happened?

Right. Tommy had tried the big, high ramp with his skateboard and he fell and really hurt himself. Rick saw Tommy being carried into the ambulance, he saw Tommy's mother crying, and then the ambulance drove off down the street.

Tommy turned out all right, but while Rick was waiting for Tommy to come home, he sat on his porch and thought about skateboards. Maybe God was trying to tell Rick something. Maybe skateboards were dangerous.

Rick watched the other kids riding their skateboards. They were all bigger than he was. Maybe six years old was too young. It would be like letting a kid in diapers try to ride a two-wheeler, he thought.

34

Finally Rick thought about his prayer to God for a skateboard. God always answers prayers, but sometimes He says no.

"Okay, God," Rick said. "If you don't want me to have a skateboard now because it's too dangerous and I'm too small that's okay. But is it all right if I ask you again next year?"

Prayer: Thank you, God, for always listening, always understanding when we pray. And thank you for not giving us what we ask for sometimes, because you love us and you know best. Amen.

14

BOW AND ARROW

Do you ever wonder what your life will be like when you grow up? What will happen?

Well, I do, too. But I heard an interesting idea. Have you ever seen a bow and arrow? (Demonstrate motions.) You pull the string way back tight, and then *zing,* the arrow shoots out.

We are like the bow and arrow, and God is the archer, the one pulling the string. God is aiming at something we can't see. He pulls the bow back, tight, tighter (demonstrate), and sometimes we say, "Ow! Hey, that hurts!" but God goes on stretching until He has His aim in sight. Then *zing*! He lets go.

We can't see what our lives are going to be like, can we? But God knows. He has a beautiful plan for each one of us. All we have to do is trust Him. We must follow what He tells us to do, love one another without being mean or hateful, and do our very best each day. Then God will work our lives out.

God loves us. Our lives are in His hands, so it is good to trust Him.

15

WARM FUZZIES
AND COLD PRICKLIES

How do you feel when someone says something nice to you, such as, "I like you; you're nice"?

It feels good, doesn't it? But now, think about how you feel when someone says something bad to you, like, "You are stupid! You did that all wrong." How does that feel? Awful! All black and prickly, like we want to get away from it.

I have here some warm fuzzies. (Hand one cotton ball to each child.) Each one of you take one of these, and when you have it in your hand, shut your eyes and feel it. Doesn't it feel soft? Rub it gently against your face. Isn't that nice? It has a warm, fuzzy feeling. This cotton ball is to remind us how it feels when someone says something nice to us, like, "You are Mommy's wonderful girl" or "You did a good job at that, son."

Now here I have a cold prickly. (Show a dried thistle.) Pass this around and shut your eyes and feel how that feels. Not so nice, hey? Try rubbing that against your face. It hurts, doesn't it? We call this a cold prickly. Keep passing it around. The cold prickly reminds us how we feel when someone says something bad to us, like, "You're ugly! I hate you!"

I want each one of you to have a warm fuzzy, but no cold prickly, because I want you to do something. Take your warm fuzzy with you and today, whenever you can, say a warm, fuzzy, nice thing to someone else. You could say, "I love you, Daddy" or "I like this dinner, Mom." Each time you see this warm, fuzzy cotton ball, or feel it in your pocket, remember to give away warm fuzzies to other people.

16

TOYS AND NO TOYS

I know a little girl, Emma, who was an only child. Her parents had plenty of money, so Emma had lots and lots of toys—every kind you can think of. One whole wall of their family room was filled with shelves of games, only she didn't often have anyone to play them with her.

So Emma was bored a lot. She would watch TV for hours, and even get tired of that. Then she would get up and wander around the back yard, wishing there were something to do.

One summer Emma visited her grandmother. Her grandmother did *not* have plenty of money. Oh, there was enough to eat, and Grandmother's house was cozy and warm, but she had almost no toys. Grandmother didn't even own a TV—just a radio.

"But what will I do all the time?" Emma asked.

"Do what you can with what you've got," her grandma said.

That didn't help Emma much. She went out and sat on the front porch and stared out at the summer day. Grandma's kitten purred up next to her. Emma patted it for a while, then the kitten jumped up to catch a dandelion seed that floated by on the breeze. That gave Emma an idea. She ran out to the grass and picked two dandelions that were all white and fluffy. Carrying them carefully, she brought them near the kitty and then shook them hard. The kitty jumped and danced all around, chasing them. Grandma heard Emma laughing with the kitty and came to watch.

Later that evening some neighbor children came over, and because there was no TV and no games to play, they invented their own, outside. It was called "chase" and they ran all over yards and yelled and tried to catch each other. Only one tree was "safe." The game was so exciting Emma could feel her heart pounding when she ran fast. She had never played like this outside. It was fun!

"Do what you can with what you have," her grandma had said. Now Emma knows it works!

17

CRUTCHES

I hurt my leg once and needed crutches. (Hold up a wooden crutch.) Did any of you ever have to use crutches? Why do we use crutches? Right, our bodies are weak and need help for a while.

Some people say, "religion is a crutch—only weak people need religion." I don't think that's right. All people have trouble. Sometimes you have trouble, sometimes I have trouble. Every single person in this room has had trouble at *some* time.

When we get in trouble, we need help. So when I hear someone say church is for weak people, people with troubles, I say, "Don't you ever have troubles?" "Well then, what crutch do you use?"

You see, everyone has troubles, and everyone also has some kind of a crutch—something to help him until he's strong again. Some people use drugs. Some people use alcohol. Some people think money will help. Some people depend on their friends when they are in trouble. This is good, but sometimes even your friends let you down.

Some people depend on themselves when they get in trouble. This doesn't always work, either; nobody's perfect.

If you are going to have help in your time of trouble, why not get the best help there is—the one Person who is perfect: God. God never wears out. And He is the most powerful helper there is. He is like a big solid rock.

41

So when you have trouble and you go to find a crutch, something to help you, don't get one that's wobbly. Get the strongest helper there is: God.

Prayer: God, we are glad that you are so strong, and that you send us some of your strength when we need it. Amen.

18

SEEING THROUGH
A GLASS DARKLY

Do you get mixed up about what people say to you? Suppose you were sitting at your kitchen table having a cup of cocoa, and your mother said, "Drink up." And then you went to visit your grandmother and had some cocoa there, and she said, "Now, drink that all down."

Well, that's confusing, isn't it?

Everybody gets mixed up sometimes, even grownups. But you know, the Bible talks about this. It says while we are here on earth, we see through a glass darkly. (Speaker holds up smoky glass, then passes it on.)* It is as if we were looking through this dark, smoky piece of glass and trying to see the world. We can't see it very clearly, can we? Here, pass this on and try to see through it to one of those bright windows there.

The Bible teaches that it is hard to see clearly what is going on while we are here on Earth; life is sometimes very confusing. But, the Bible *promises* us something! When we die and go home to be with God, then we will see clearly. (Pass around clear glass or plexiglass, similarly taped for safety.) Life will be as clear and as beautiful as those colors in the window, and we will understand it all.

*Spray paint a piece of plexiglass or glass and tape edges with masking tape for safe handling.

Prayer: Thank you, God, for your clear promise of heaven: and while we are here on earth if we get confused, help us walk with you, holding your hand. Amen.

19

THE SMASHED PAPER CUP

I know a six-year-old boy named Billy who doesn't like to come to church.

He doesn't like to come to church because he has to get all dressed up in a stiff shirt. And whenever he barely moves in his pew, people shush him up and tell him to sit still. One lady even turned around from the pew in front of him and frowned a very bad frown-face at Billy, just because he kicked the back of her pew by accident.

In his church school room, the students cut out pictures and listened to stories, but the scissors were stiff and hard to work, and the girl next to Billy kept pinching him. Billy just didn't like church and he didn't see why he had to come.

Even though Billy complained about church, his parents insisted that he come. Things went on like this, but one week his parents said they were not only going to church on Sunday, but on Wednesday nights, too! You can imagine how Billy felt about that.

Actually, Wednesday night wasn't too bad. Billy got to eat a lot of food, especially desserts. He liked that. He had three colors of jello and four different kinds of chocolate cake. Things were going pretty well until someone blew a whistle and the dinner part was over. Billy was pushed into one corner of the room where a lot of people sat on the floor, and he was supposed to sit with them. Where were his parents? They were far across the room.

Billy's forehead got all wrinkled up and he put his head down. He didn't like being with a bunch of strange people.

Some man in his group held up some paper cups. (Speaker holds up paper cups.) "We're going to play a kind of game tonight," he said.

"Oh, no," thought Billy.

"This is the church," said the man, holding up a paper cup. "Each person is to take one and make it the way he wants his church to be."

Billy thought, "Oh, brother, what am I supposed to do? This is a dumb game."

"And let's have a rule of silence while we play this game," the man said.

"That's just like church," thought Billy. "We always have to be quiet!"

He watched the first lady take the paper cup and do this (speaker demonstrates): she tore little strips out from the center of the cup.

The next person took another cup, tore a cross shape out of it, and taped it on the first cup.

Nobody said anything. The whole room was quiet.

Billy saw the cross on the paper cup and remembered it meant the church. It was supposed to mean loving, caring for people. But Billy sure didn't feel loving now. Yipes, it was almost his turn! He didn't know what to do. This was awful! They would all think he was stupid. He wished he could go over and be with his parents.

Oops, there was the cup, handed to him. Dumb ole church. Billy took the cup and crumpled it and slammed it down on the floor (speaker demonstrates).

Billy sat and glared at his dusty shoes. After awhile he heard crunching and crackling near by. When he peeked, it was the teenage boy next to him, carefully unfolding Billy's smashed cup.

The teenager looked at Billy as he fixed the cup. He looked kind, like he wanted to help Billy out. In fact, he was being so careful it looked like he was helping that poor smashed paper cup just as much as he wanted to help Billy (speaker unfolds crumpled paper cup).

When the cup was all cup-shape again, the teenager untaped the cross and put it inside, as though he wanted to put the love of God inside Billy. Then he looked at Billy and smiled.

Billy was surprised. Wasn't everybody mad at him?

The group soon ended and the teenager whispered to Billy that someone had just put out another chocolate cake and no one else had seen it yet. So they sneaked over and ate some. Pretty soon Billy began to feel better, and later he was even laughing. You see, Billy saw why coming to church is important: people here have something *loving* to teach you!

Prayer: Dear Father, help us learn why we should come to church. Help us learn to be loving to other people. Amen.

20

THE ESCALATORS

Who knows what escalators are?

That's right. They are like moving stairways, and you find them in big stores or airports.

How many of you have learned to ride on an escalator?

Then you know it is easier to ride on one when you are holding onto someone's hand, like your mom's or your dad's hand, right?

I want to tell you about a boy named Brian. He had just learned to ride the escalator with his mother and dad. He was pretty scared when they first did it. As they rode down, his mother said, "Now get your foot up, get ready to step off." He never seemed to be quite ready and he stumbled when he got off, but his mother's hand always held him up. He used to worry that something terrible would happen to him if he didn't step off the escalator just right. But nothing ever did.

After awhile he got better and better at riding escalators. And he got braver about them. One day, he and his mother were in the store. His mother was wandering off, looking at other things, and she said, "You be good now, Brian."

His mother wasn't looking, so Brian thought, "I think I will try riding this escalator all by myself."

The only problem was that the escalator was coming down, down, down in front of Brian. So, how could he ride it?

Well, he tried. He took a big step up and *bump,* he was right back down where he started. *Huh,* he thought, *this wasn't the way it worked when I rode the escalator with Dad.* So he tried again. He took a big step up, then *bump,* he was right back where he started. Maybe he'd better try a little harder. So he did. He took two big steps up as fast as his legs could climb. Well, you know what happened again, don't you? He came right back down.

Brian was a stubborn, hard working kid, so he kept at it. After awhile he got to where he could run up four or five steps before he was returned down.

But he had problems. Sometimes big people were riding down, and when he tried to run up past them, they got in his way. One lady even swatted him with her shopping bag! He tried to hold on to the railings with his hand to help pull himself up, but those railings were moving down, *too,* just like the escalator was always moving down.

Well, that's where I came in. I was walking by in that store and saw Brian trying to run up that escalator that was moving down. Poor Brian, he was working so hard. His face was all red and he was puffing and sweaty and his shirttail was hanging out, and I could see he was getting mad.

That sometimes happens to us. We try to be good. We try hard to work our way up, but before we know it—if we rest a minute—we are right back down where we started. We have to keep working all the time to be good, just like Brian's legs had to keep running all the time on that escalator. If he stood still for a second, he would be right back down where he started.

I see a lot of people running, running, all the time, trying so hard to be good, and I think *Wait a minute. This isn't right. This isn't the way God meant our lives to be. He wouldn't expect us to wear ourselves out being good.*

I watched Brian, because now his mom and dad had come. They were talking to him, calming him down, listening to him. Then they took his hand and went around the corner (significant pause). They went to the other escalator—the one that went up.

The last time I saw Brian, he was riding smoothly up, looking out all over the store, holding his father's hand. He sure looked happy!

God wants to show us the right way to be good. He wants to take our hand and help us. He never meant for it to be so hard to be good, like Brian running and puffing on the wrong escalator. So whenever you find yourself having trouble, when you are trying hard and it's not working out, remember Brian and the escalators. Stop and take God your Father's hand and pray. Talk to Him. Let God show you the easier way, the right way.

21

LOST IN THE SUPERMARKET

Has anyone here ever been lost in the grocery store?

How does it feel when you realize you are lost?

Yes, you're afraid, aren't you? I know, because I was a child once and I got lost, too.

When we realize we are lost, we get scared, our heart beats faster, and we breathe faster (speaker breathes fast, almost panting, with eyes wide), and we rush around looking. We feel like running fast and yelling, "Help! Help!" We wish we had never come to the supermarket. We tear around and feel like crying, and all the places we run seem so big that we feel all alone.

But now, think about how it feels to be found. Suppose you have been running all over the supermarket, crying, and a lady helps you look for your mother, and pretty soon you see her. You run down the aisle to her and get a big hug.

How does that feel?

That's right. It's wonderful. Jesus knew all about being lost and being found. And He told us a wonderful secret that can help us when we are lost: "Lo, I am with you always, even unto the end of the world."

You know what that means?

Jesus is always near you, even though you can't see Him. Even if you don't pay any attention to Him, He is still there. So you never really are alone. You have a wonderful friend who is always with you.

Prayer: Jesus, thank you for being our friend, and for always being with us. Amen.

22

THREE HUGS A DAY

I know a family that has a rule: "Everybody needs three hugs a day." Did you ever hear of that? How about your family—do you hug a lot?

Of course, you have to hug at the right times, not when your father is driving a car, and it probably isn't a good idea to hug while you are riding an escalator. Right?

This family always got a good morning hug before breakfast. It started the day right, making them feel all warm and cozy and happy. The kids got hugged "welcome home" from school, too. And they always hugged the father "welcome home" when he came home from work. They hugged goodbye when they went away and they hugged hello when they came back. They got hugged when they did a good job or when they scraped their knees. Even the mother and daddy got hugs at times when she made an especially good dinner or when he made a bookcase.

This was a very happy family. But one day, the littlest girl in the family got sick. Her parents took her to the hospital and the doctors put her under a clear plastic tent to help her breathing. She could see out of the clear plastic, like a person can see through glass, and she saw her mother right there next to her, but she couldn't touch her. She felt lonesome. The little girl was sick for a long time but she finally got better, and she was very glad when they took the plastic tent off and she could get a nice big hug from her mother again.

A long time after the little girl came home, her father got the sniffles. He took a glass of orange juice, his briefcase, and his Kleenex and went to bed. No one saw him all day. Finally at night, the little girl opened his door just a little bit, peeked in and said, "Daddy?"

He looked very grumpy. He had work papers spread all over his bed and he looked like his head hurt. The little girl came in anyway. She carefully pushed aside the work papers, climbed onto the bed and gave her daddy a big squeeze. Then she whispered, "Everybody needs three hugs a day."

And you know what? Her daddy felt better!

So, if your family doesn't know this, why don't you tell them: "Everybody needs three hugs a day." And you begin by giving the first hug!

Prayer: Father, we know that Jesus welcomed the little children and said, "Forbid them not." Help melt any stiffness within us. Help us learn to hug more and let your love flow through our arms and out to your people around us. Amen.

23

THE STUMP THAT SPROUTED

Once when I was walking in the country I saw where a tree had just been cut down. All that was left was a stump. Have any of you seen a stump? Then you know what I mean: it used to be a big tree, but now it is just cut flat across the top (indicate low height with hand) and a person can sit on it.

This tree stump I saw had just been been freshly sawed down. I could see that the wood was new and the sap was running out of it. *Oh, too bad,* I thought when I saw it. *I wonder why it was cut down.*

It looked like it had been a big, strong tree. The stump was this wide (indicate with hands two feet apart). What had happened to make it be cut down? Maybe lightning hit it and it got all split apart. Have any of you ever seen a tree that has been hit by lightning?

Or maybe the tree was sick and had to be cut down. Trees get sick just like we do, you know. Or, maybe it was cut down because a new road was being built right where the tree stood. There could be lots of reasons why it was cut down.

A year later I was walking in the same place in the country and I saw the same stump. It was older now. It was sort of black on top and no sap was running down. But do you know what I saw? Five green twigs were growing right up out of the stump!

Boy, look at that! I thought. *Isn't nature something? Here you think you've killed a tree by cutting it down, and five new little trees grow out of the old one.*

And I thought about how much bigger and bushier the new trees would be. They will probably be this wide (spread arms wide) and have lots of places for birds to nest again.

Sometimes we have trouble and feel like we have been chopped down. We feel like that tree stump. But then, little by little, we come back. And even though it may take a long time, we turn out better!

Prayer: God, please stay with us in our times of trouble, so, like that tree, we come back even stronger. Amen.

24

THANKSGIVING BUBBLEGUM

Today is Thanksgiving Sunday, and on Thanksgiving we think about what we are thankful for. Right? I know a family that hangs a great big long roll of paper from the ceiling, all down one wall, and on this long roll of paper they write all the things they are thankful for. It is a really long list! Any time someone in the family thinks of something else, they go in, take the pencil on a string next to the paper, and write it down. They've kept the list for years, rolling it up and writing more on the bottom each Thanksgiving. They can see how many things they have to thank God for. It makes them feel really blessed by God.

Some people don't feel thankful on Thanksgiving, though. Maybe they think they have good reason: they have no turkey dinner with stuffing, or maybe someone is missing from the table this year, so they feel sad. Maybe they are sick, or there isn't enough money. It's hard to be thankful when you are feeling sad or lonely or grumpy.

I have a story about this. Once the Greenfield family went camping. They camped near the shore of the ocean, and every night before they went to bed they all took a long walk along the beach, right at the edge of the ocean.

Their bare feet felt the wet sand and the waves sliding in. They could see lots and lots of stars over their heads. They walked a long, long way; it was their favorite time together.

The only problem they had on these walks was that four-year-old Marcy's legs got tired and she couldn't keep up. So her Daddy carried her piggy-back. Do you know what that is? Have any of you been carried piggy-back? Okay, then you know what's it like.

They all walked along the sand, Marcy bouncing along up high and her daddy complaining, "You are really getting heavy, Marcy. Are you sure you aren't picking up rocks back there?"

Marcy laughed and said no. And her daddy kept trudging through the sand—trudge, trudge, trudge. "Boy," he puffed, "you are really lucky to be carried along like this."

"You are lucky too, Daddy," Marcy said into his ear.

"Oh, yeah? Why am I so lucky?" he said as he trudged along.

"You are lucky, Daddy, because I have some bubblegum in my mouth, and I am not blowing it into your hair!"

You see, sometimes we never know how fortunate we are. So if there ever is a Thanksgiving when you don't feel very thankful, or any time when you are sad or lonely or grumpy, start making a list. Write down one thing after another you are grateful for. If you can't write yet, think them out loud (hold up one finger for each item). You probably are glad you have a mom or dad who loves you. Maybe you are glad you have enough to eat and clothes to wear. You are grateful for a cozy bed, and maybe for one special stuffed animal you like. You are grateful for your dog or cat. You are glad you can see the sun and trees. Once you get started, the list gets bigger and bigger.

So let's remember Thanksgiving bubblegum: let's make ourselves aware of all the things we take for granted, yet are grateful for.

25

THE BIRDS AND THE BLIZZARD
(Christmas)

I have a friend named Jennifer. One evening she was waiting for her parents to come home, but there was a snowstorm outside, and they were taking longer than they expected.

Jennifer stood at her living room picture window, looking for them (peering gesture) when Thump! (jump back) something hit the glass right next to her!

It really surprised Jennifer. I bet it would surprise you, too, wouldn't it?

You know what it was? It was a bird, flying into the glass window. Jennifer could just barely see it now, out on the snow, not moving.

The poor bird! Jennifer thought, *I'd better go out and get it. Maybe it has broken a wing or something.* So she grabbed her jacket and boots and as she was putting them on, she heard two more *thumps!*

She jumped up and went to see. Yep, two more birds lay unmoving on the snow. That wasn't good, was it? So she hurried outside and when she got there, there were even more thumps, more birds flying, banging into the glass.

Why did they do that? Jennifer looked up and saw the cold snow whirling around her and the bright warm light in the picture window. Of course! They saw that and wanted to come and get warm.

And they couldn't see the window glass! They didn't know the danger.

What should she do? They were still banging into the glass. She ran up and waved her arms around, calling, "No, no! Go away!" But the birds only scattered and fluttered and kept coming back.

Then she had an idea: she ran into the house and turned off the living room lights. There! They quit banging into the picture window. But now what did she hear? Bangs into the *kitchen* glass! Why, the birds were trying everywhere there was a warm light! So Jennifer ran all through the house, turning off the lights in each room.

Then she ran outside to see if the birds were all right now. They were wheeling and flying around, all confused, not knowing where to go. The snow was getting worse.

Then she had another idea: she could turn on a light in the barn and open the door so the birds could fly in and be warm. And that's what she did. A few birds saw the light and flew in right away. But when she ran back to the front picture window, the rest of the birds couldn't see the barn's light. It was behind the house. And, some of the birds were still banging into the picture window, because they remembered it had looked warm.

Jennifer was so frustrated she almost stamped her feet and yelled *I wish I could become a bird and speak their language,* she thought. *I'd tell them where the light and the warm place is.*

And then something occurred to her: that's why Jesus came.

God became one of us, to speak our language and to tell us where the light and warmth and safety is.

The storm blew over. Jennifer had helped many of the birds, but the thing she never forgot was how she stood in the snow and suddenly understood why Jesus came to us.

26

BLACKOUT AT TOM's HOUSE

I know a boy about your age who had a power failure—a blackout—at his house. Who knows what happens during a blackout? Have any of you ever been home during a blackout?

Tom was at home one evening and everything was normal. Almost everything, that is. Tom had had an awful day at school. He hadn't finished his schoolwork, so the teacher made him bring it home.

Tom was sitting in the kitchen doing his schoolwork and he was really upset about it because he didn't understand it. He couldn't even take time out to watch TV (substitute the name of an early evening TV program).

There he was sitting at the kitchen table when suddenly all the lights went out!

"Hey!" his brother yelled, "the TV went off!"

"Dear me," his mother said, "the water was running in the sink and I can't see a thing!"

It was really dark. "Don't worry, kids, the power has just gone off," Tom's dad said, feeling his way into the kitchen. "It will probably come right back on."

So Tom and his brother and his parents waited a minute or two, but it was still dark.

Do you know what Tom thought, sitting there in the dark kitchen?

"God, it is awful dark in here. This is kinda scary, God. Oh, and I have all this homework, too, and I don't even know how to do it. This whole day has been rotten. Do you think you could please help, God?"

Well, it was dark for a long, long time. "Here are some candles," his mother said. "We can at least see until the lights go back on."

While they waited, the family decided to build a fire in the fireplace. Tom and his brother snuggled into sleeping bags on their living room rug in front of the fire. Tom was all cozy.

His dad couldn't read his magazine, and the stove didn't work for his mom, so they joined the cozy ones in front of the fireplace. Tom's parents told the boys stories about when they were kids. "Wow!" Tom said, "this is fun!"

The best part came when his mom remembered the old popcorn pan in the basement. They put popcorn in it and cooked it over the fire, and drank Coke.

So, there were candles all over, a fire, and sleeping bags; they were camping out in their own living room!

Tom never did get his schoolwork done that night. But it was all right because his teacher had been in the blackout, too, and she excused the kids from all homework.

The blackout turned into a very special time with his family that Tom always remembered.

Prayer: Dear Father, help us remember that trouble is high adventure with God. Amen.

27

TRAFFIC SIGNS

(Hold up stop sign) Who can tell me what this is? Right, a stop sign. What does it tell people to do?

Sometimes a policeman holds up a stop sign like this (stand up) and lets kids walk across the street from school. (Demonstrate waving kids across the street with your free hand.) The stop sign tells the drivers to wait, so all those kids won't be run over.

How about this traffic light—see how the green is bright? What does the green tell you to do? Go. Green for go, red for stop.

Have you ever seen a sign like this? Who knows what it is? A speed limit sign. It means you can drive your car only fifty-five miles per hour, no faster. Why do we have signs like this? Do you think your parents ever drive a little bit faster than the speed limit?

Well, sometimes I do, too. It's hard to obey the signs all the time, but I do try to do just what the signs say because I know these are good things for car drivers. They remind drivers of the rules. And if everyone obeys the rules for driving a car, no one gets hurt.

But what if there were no rules for driving a car? (Put signs down with a clatter.) Suppose we took all the signs down and said, "That's okay, everybody; no more rules! Everyone can drive any way he wants!" What would happen? That's right, it would be a mess. Your best friend might get run over, or your mom or dad might get killed in a car crash—it would be awful!

So rules are a good thing to have. They make driving a car better for everyone.

Did you know God made some rules? (Sit back down among the kids.) Not about driving, but about how to live your life. There are ten big ones. Does anyone know what they are called? Right, the Ten Commandments.

God's people Israel were having an awful time. They were taking a long, long walk through a desert—a dry, dusty place where there was nothing to eat and very little water to drink. This was such a long walk it took over forty *years*! Anyway, these people would camp out at night, but they weren't very good campers. They had left their homes in such a hurry that they didn't have time to pack much. Some people didn't have any tents or food or matches. The people began to grumble and fight and things got worse and worse and worse. Lots of people wanted to go back, even after they had come such a long way.

God looked down on them and saw them squabbling and having an awful time, so He gave Moses, their leader, ten rules. He carved them into stone, gave them to Moses, and said, "Teach the people to follow these rules, and things will go much better."

And you know, God was right! Whenever people carefully followed these ten rules, their lives were happier and better. The rules worked so well that all of the countries of the Western world made them into law—the laws we live by.

For instance, one of the Ten Commandments is "Thou shalt not murder." If you asked a policeman, "Is it against the law to kill someone?" what would he say?

Some people don't like rules. Rules *are* hard to obey, and everyone feels like ignoring the rules sometimes. But just remember: God's rules are good ones. They help everyone be happier. If you don't follow His rules, life can be like everyone driving crazy and crashing into each other.

Prayer: Dear Father, we know you are bigger and much wiser than us. We thank you for giving us the Ten Commandments, for showing us the way to live a good and happy life. Amen.

28

CELEBRATING WOMEN

Did you ever stop to think that half the people in the world are girls or women? I want to tell you about two, and they are both named Harriet.

The first Harriet, Harriet Tubman, was born about one hundred-fifty years ago in this country as a slave. There were lots of black slaves then, and, like many of them, Harriet did hard work out in the fields every day. She wasn't allowed to go to school like you.

Harriet hoed crops and hauled and lifted things, working outdoors and growing strong. People used to say she could pick up a man, sling him over her shoulder, and walk off down the road with him.

But she didn't like being a slave. So one night Harriet Tubman ran away from her slave home to the North, where she could be free.

Now, about this time, another woman named Harriet was also thinking slavery was not right. This Harriet was Harriet Beecher Stowe. She had seven preachers in her family. Each Sunday she would sit in her pew in church and hear them preach that each person was made by God and was special in himself. No one should have to be a slave. "That's right," she would think, "slaves should be free, but what can I do to help? I'm not a preacher." She wasn't a preacher, but God had given this Harriet one special talent: she was a good storyteller.

So this Harriet wrote a very exciting story. She told how awful it was to be a slave and how much slaves wanted to escape to freedom. Harriet's story was made into a book called *Uncle Tom's Cabin* and it sold thousands and thousands of copies. Pretty soon everyone in America was talking about it.

Probably even Harriet Tubman, our slave girl who ran away North, heard about the story. While she had been in the North, she had been thinking. Her life was better as a free person. She decided she would go back and help some of her people escape to the North, to Canada, so that they could be free, too.

This was dangerous. Runaway slaves could be shot, even killed. But Harriet Tubman knew it was so important to be free, she helped slaves escape anyway. You see, God had given this Harriet something special, too—courage. She was very brave and very smart. She was also very strong, because she had to walk all the way from the South to the far North, and she did it hundreds of times.

Through the dark of night Harriet would lead her people, running miles and miles, night after night, to the North, to freedom. They couldn't take main roads because someone might see them. So they had to go through fields and woods. They kept looking for the north star, following it north to freedom.

It must have been scary. But Harriet Tubman and her people had some surprising help. Harriet Beecher Stowe's book made lots of people think. They decided slavery was wrong, too, so they helped Harriet Tubman and her escaping slaves.

Every day people opened their houses to the escaping slaves, gave them food and a safe place to sleep. Soon there were such secret houses all along the way from the South to North. Each stop was called a station on the Underground Railroad.

This Underground Railroad wasn't all underground and it wasn't a railroad. It was a group of people secretly helping slaves run North to freedom.

Harriet Tubman led more than three hundred of her people North to freedom, and every one of them arrived safely. She drew maps of the way on dirt floors, so thousands more could come on their own, helped by the Underground Railroad. Harriet became so famous they called her Moses, after the Moses in the Bible who also led his people out of slavery from Egypt.

These two women, Harriet Beecher Stowe and Harriet Tubman, each had special talents and God used their special talents to help people. In fact, God uses women all over our country, all over the world to help people.

Prayer: Dear Father, thank you for the girls and women in your world. Thank you for their talents and help us to look around at the women in our lives and tell them how wonderful they are, too. Amen.

Suggestion: Cut out two-inch red felt hearts and give one to each child at the end of this story to help them remember the courageous hearts of these women.

29

JIMMY'S COZY BED

I know a boy named Jimmy who is about your age. Every morning before he has to get up, he wakes up a few minutes early and enjoys snuggling under the warm covers. He curls up in a ball with his covers pulled up around his ears and he feels cozy.

A few mornings ago he was thinking while he was all snuggled up like this, "I bet this is how my new baby brother feels, right before he is born."

You see, Jimmy was going to have a new baby brother or sister in his family, soon. Everyone in the family was looking forward to the baby coming. Jimmy's mother told him it would be any day now.

Jimmy wondered, though, if the *baby* was looking forward to coming. When you think about it, being born is quite a shock. A baby has to leave a cozy warm place and come into a chilly hospital room, with bright lights, loud noises, and he even has his bottom spanked! No wonder newborn babies yell; they don't like the change.

Snuggled down in his warm bed, Jimmy decided being born was kind of like having to get out of bed on a cold morning. You would much rather stay where you are safe and warm. Jimmy wondered what would happen if he stayed in bed for the rest of his life. He thought about all the things he would miss: good food, his birthday party, the trip to Disney World, playing outside. . . . So he jumped out of bed and got dressed.

Early the next morning Jimmy again snuggled under the covers. He didn't want to get out of bed. His baby brother didn't want to be born, either. His Grandpa was sick, but he didn't want to die. All three were in sort of the same situation.

Jimmy's grandpa didn't want to leave this safe world that he was used to. None of us wants to. We feel like yelling "No! No!" just like when we have to jump out of bed.

None of us wants to change, to go to a new place that seems scary and different. But should we really be afraid to die and go to heaven?

Jesus promised us that He was going to prepare a place for us. Why should we be afraid to join Him in a new life in heaven?

It *is* quite a change. But someone we already know will be there to welcome us, and it is a wonderful place.

So this morning Jimmy decided that when his time came, he wouldn't be afraid to go to heaven. He jumped out of bed and had a great day!

30

ANNE AND KATHY

Do any of you have some smaller kids in your neighborhood that you help or take care of sometimes?

I want to tell you a story about a girl named Anne. She had a neighbor girl named Kathy who was almost two years old (speaker indicates two-year-old height with hand). Anne was a lot older than Kathy (speaker indicates eight-year-old height) but she really liked little Kathy anyway. Lots of times after school Anne would take Kathy for rides in her wagon around the driveway. Or sometimes Anne would lift Kathy up onto the swing and push her very gently. Anne was careful with Kathy because she was so little. Kathy would toddle out to the street and Anne would run and take her hand and bring her back onto the grass.

One day Anne came into her own house giggling, and her mother asked her what had happened.

"That Kathy—she's so *cute*! You know what she did? We were playing in the sandbox and she started eating the sand, so I said, 'No, no, Kathy. No eat sand.' So she brought her shovel over and began to feed the sand to me! So I said, 'No, no, Kathy. Annie no eat sand.' And then she put her shovel down and gave me a big hug!"

Anne and her mother smiled, thinking about it. "I sure do like little Kathy," Anne said. "She is just darling."

Then her mother said, "You know what, Anne? God loves you just like you love little Kathy. He thinks you are *so* cute, and He really enjoys it when you are loving. You are His darling, too!"

Anne was surprised. "You mean God thinks I'm as cute as Kathy?"

"Yep."

"But I'm not, really. She is much cuter."

"God doesn't think so. He loves every hair on your head. He loves you like *crazy*!"

"Does He really? How do you know?"

"I just know."

Anne thought about that a long time, for years in fact. It seemed hard to believe that God loved her that much. But it's true. God loves you like crazy, too. He really does.

Prayer: Lord, help us learn to see how much you love us. Thank you for all that love.

31

THE SIMPLE LIFE

Once there was a young newly-married couple named Sue and John. They didn't have much money, but they loved each other and were happy to be together. They lived in a little cottage back off a dirt lane. It certainly wasn't like the houses we live in; it didn't even have a bathroom. But Sue and John had high hopes and they prayed for prosperity.

John was a cabinet-maker—a carpenter who makes cabinets and furniture. Sue loved to sit in John's woodworking room and smell the good sawdust smells and watch him. And while she watched, Sue could crochet lace, very delicate, beautiful lace.

So they spent their days together, John woodworking and Sue lace-making, and they enjoyed long talks as they worked and strolls outside after lunch. They always had their coffee by the fire in late afternoon. Theirs was a cozy life.

John was paid well for his woodworking because he did a fine job. Sue saved up the money she made for her lace, which was much in demand among the fine ladies of the land. Sue would take her money and buy something special for John, like a bright red velvet vest for him to wear to church. And John would save out some of his money and buy a surprise for Sue, like a small golden locket. She put it on and never took it off. On Sundays they would take long walks across the meadow in back of their cottage, smell the fresh air and delight in the flowers, and thank God that things were so wonderful for them. And they would pray for prosperity to smile on them.

And do you know what happened? They did begin to prosper. One especially good year, John announced that they could now afford a maid to help Sue with the housework. Sue was surprised, because there was only one room in the cottage, but it was nice to have someone around to help.

Only now when John was in his woodworking room, Sue followed the maid around, making sure she dusted under the beds and weeded the garden correctly. John missed Sue, missed the long talks with her as he worked, and missed her surprise hugs and kisses in the middle of the day. (They couldn't giggle and kiss in front of the maid, could they?) So, John and Sue waited until the maid went home every night, and then they had their talks. And that was okay—for a while.

Soon John prospered even more, and he decided that the time had come to move out of the small cottage to a real honest-to-goodness house. So they did. And at the house, they needed a housekeeper who lived right there, plus a cook.

Years went by. John's cabinet-making grew into a big business with many men working with John to make cabinets. Everyone prospered. John and Sue now had a very big house with a housekeeper, a cook, three maids, and a gardener. And Sue missed John, because she hardly ever saw him. She spent the whole day settling quarrels among the people who worked around the house, and it was all getting pretty complicated. Sue frequently got angry, and in one of her tempers, demanded that she have her own lace-maker. After all, what was the good of all this money she and John had, if she couldn't enjoy it? So Sue got her own lace-maker, and her own corset-hooker-upper.

Now their house was so large it was a mansion with miles of land around it and goats and sheep to tend. So they hired goat tenders and cheese-makers and farmer overseers, and laundry maids and ironing ladies as well as the whole staff in the big house. In fact, 387 people now worked for John and Sue, and their mansion was

73

so huge that one whole side of it was for Sue and her maids and ladies and the other side for John and his groomsmen and billiard rooms and offices.

One day Sue was sitting on the third sitting porch to the left of the library with a cup of tea, and she looked out over the green fields and saw the goat tender. He was swinging down the meadow, holding hands with the daughter of the cheese-maker. The two of them were in love and were going to be married that Sunday and live in a small cottage near the back of Sue's property.

Sue looked at them walking along barefoot, just enjoying the sunny day, with nothing more to bother them than taking care of the herd of goats. And Sue envied them. She wished she and John were there, barefoot, just the two of them, walking down the grass.

So, is the moral of this story that money is always bad? No, having lots of money can be nice.

The moral of this story is that we had better be careful what we pray for. Sometimes God gives us what we ask for, but things don't turn out quite like we planned. In fact, we discover we were better off before, yet never noticed it!

So, when you pray, look at your life and try to figure out what is most important to you. What was most important to Sue and John was that they loved each other and were together, working side by side, sharing their lives closely.

I wonder what would have happened if they had prayed for love in their lives and to be able to stay close together.

Prayer: Dear God, help us to see that your plan is better than anything we could dream up for ourselves. Help us learn to trust you. Amen.

32

INVISIBLE FRIENDS

When I was learning to drive a car someone told me that when I was driving the car around by myself, I should pretend that I had an invisible policeman riding on the trunk of the car. If I pretended that he was there, I would always drive carefully, the way I should, because he would be watching me.

Do all invisible friends tell us to be good and remind us when we are bad? A real friend is fun to be with, isn't he? He likes us and is kind to us.

Before Jesus died and went to heaven, He told us that He would send His Holy Spirit to be with us. There are three parts to God: God the Father, Jesus the Son of God, and the Holy Spirit. The Holy Spirit is like an invisible friend. Another name for the Holy Spirit is "the Comforter," and I like that. It sounds nice, doesn't it?

Every person in this room has times when he could use a comforter, someone to help him feel more comfortable. What is this Holy Spirit, this Comforter like? You can't see Him; He is invisible. But you can feel His presence inside you.

As you learn about God and get to know Him as a friend, it's nice to be able to talk to Him whenever you feel like it. For instance, you might say something to Him like, "I am having a hard time doing this scissors work, Friend. Did you ever have to go to kindergarten?"

You can tell your invisible Friend what you are afraid of, you can tell Him when you feel happy, you can tell Him anything. And because He is part of God, He will always listen, He will comfort and love you.

Prayer: Thank you, Father, for the gift of your Holy Spirit. Help us to learn to talk to our Comforter. Amen.

33

TWO STICKS IN
THE STREAM

Have any of you ever gone wading in a small stream of water? Not the ocean, but a little river, where the water goes around rocks and branches?

Once there was a little girl named Donna who was wading in a small stream behind her house. It was a nice warm day and the sun was shining and one would think Donna would be enjoying herself.

But Donna was very sad. Her father had packed his suitcases and moved out of their house that day. Donna's mother said they were getting a divorce.

Donna found two sticks, a big one and a little one. "I know," she thought, "I'll drop these in the water and if they stay together, then it will be like my daddy and I will stay together, even though he has moved out of our house.

Donna decided to try this little game with her sticks. The big stick would be her pretend daddy and the little stick would be like herself.

So she carefully dropped them into the flowing water, trying to aim them in the middle of the stream so they wouldn't get stuck on any rocks.

But uh, oh. Donna's little stick got caught on a bunch of branches and old grass, and her father's stick floated away by itself down the stream.

"Oh, no!" she whispered, and climbed out of the water and ran along the edge, following the big stick. Where was it? She couldn't even see it! Oh, wait, there it was. The big stick that was her pretend daddy had floated far away, and now he, too, was stuck, trapped by a rock.

Donna ran back to her little stick. It was still stuck in the branches. There they were: Donna and her daddy, far apart, both stuck.

"I wish I'd never played this game," Donna thought, and felt even sadder (speaker frowns).

Then she remembered something she had heard right here in church: when you are in trouble or when you are feeling sad, ask God to help.

So, Donna whispered, "Please God, help me. Everything is awful."

And guess what happened? A little wind blew Donna's hair and rustled the branches. And Donna's small stick loosened. "C'mon little stick" Donna said. "You can do it!" As she watched, her little stick got looser and looser and broke free from the twigs and dry grass and was floating down the stream.

Donna hopped out of the water to watch it, and the little stick was moving faster now. It bumped right into the big stick that was stuck by the rock! Now they were both loose!

"This game is going better, now," thought Donna. There were both sticks, floating along side by side, getting a little stuck here and there, but still moving.

"I think I'll stop here," decided Donna. "I don't want to follow the sticks too far and see where they go."

So Donna went back into her house and told her mother about her game with the two sticks. Her mother understood about games like that. She told Donna again that even though her daddy had moved out of their house, Donna would still see him a lot. He would come over every weekend and call her frequently.

We don't *lose* people we love, just because they leave.

Well, that's the way it worked out for Donna. It was pretty hard, getting used to the divorce, but Donna did see her father a lot. He came to visit every weekend and he called her on the phone. He never stopped loving her and Donna never stopped loving him.

Prayer: Dear God, please help us with the big changes in our lives. Amen.

34

NURSERY ROOM WINDOW

I know a girl named Laurie, who had a little sister named Beth. Laurie thought her little sister was a real pest. Laurie's mom kept telling her to be nice to her sister because she was so little. That was hard because Laurie's sister broke her favorite toys and was always following her around.

One day Laurie's mom drove up to Beth's nursery school and said, "Laurie, get out of the car and go get Beth and bring her out here."

So Laurie went up to the nursery school door like a big girl, only the door was shut. Laurie pulled and pulled but she couldn't get it open. She didn't know what to do, but then she noticed something: in the window right next to the door she could see into the nursery school room—and there was Beth. But what was this? Beth was not the only one in the room. There was a little boy with her. And as Laurie watched, he grabbed Beth's crayon drawing and ripped it! Then he crumpled it up! Laurie saw Beth crying and stamping her feet. Laurie felt mad. Poor Beth! To have her picture wrecked like that! Laurie wanted to jump right through the glass to help Beth.

She saw Beth trying to smooth out the picture. Beth slowly carried the ruined picture over to the wastebasket and put it in. She looked so sad. Laurie felt sad, too.

Here came the nursery school teacher. She was stuffing Beth into her coat, rushing her. Beth tried to show the teacher her ruined picture, but the teacher was too busy. Laurie saw Beth wipe her eyes with the back of her hand (speaker demonstrates), and then the door opened and the nursery school kids noisily came out.

Laurie found Beth near the end of the line coming out the door. She took Beth's hand and led her to the car.

Their mother made an angry face at Beth: "What took you so long? We are going to be late! Hurry up and get in!"

The door slammed and they all drove off. Beth sat in the back seat, trying hard not to cry. Laurie looked over at her, thinking, "I know just how she feels."

Laurie saw Beth with feelings, just like hers: crying feelings, angry feelings, lonesome feelings. As soon as Laurie saw this, she and Beth became friends. And they have been friends ever since.

35

JOB'S FOOTPRINTS

(Ahead of time cut out a set of men's footprints from paper and tape them visibly in front of the church—up the aisle, across a wall, down the lectern, etc. Alongside the large footprints, tape medium-size footprints, only leave several areas where the large ones are alone.)

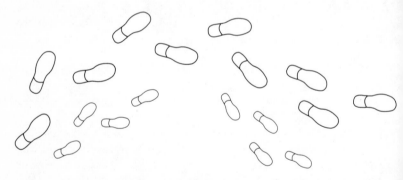

What are all these footprints here for? They are part of our story today. Has anyone ever heard of Job, from the Bible? Job was a good man; he never cheated, never lied or did anything wrong, but do you know what? All of a sudden bad things began to happen to Job.

"Why?" he wondered. "Why were all these bad things happening to him?" In just one day, he lost all his money and his family died. Then, he got sick with sores all over his body, like giant chicken pox. Has anyone here ever had chicken pox? It's no fun, is it?

What are some other awful things you can think of besides chicken pox? How about when your dog dies? Or when your friend moves away? (Wait for children to suggest others: the flu, parents get a divorce, etc.)

Well, these things are all real troubles and we wonder why such bad things happen. This man Job wondered, too. He knew about God, and he knew for certain that God loved him, yet why all these troubles?

It's a mystery, isn't it? (Shake head. Pause.)

When you get home, have your mom or dad read you the story of Job, maybe from your children's Bible. It helps with this mystery. But for now, remember three things (hold up one finger for each item):

1. *Trouble is a part of life.* Everyone has troubles at some time or other. We may not understand why, but God is very great and He knows what He is doing. So, that's one: trouble is a part of life.

2. *God does love us.* Even in the middle of our troubles, He looks down on us and loves us and wants to comfort and help us. So, that's two: God does love us.

3. *God will never leave us.* Once someone had a dream that helped explain this. He dreamed that he was walking along the beach with God. (Speaker gets up and steps along the footprints on the floor.) As he walked along the beach with God, all around him were scenes from his own life, like little movies. Over there was the time his dog died (gesture to one corner) and there was his first day at school, and there was the time he was sick. And in each scene he noticed two sets of footprints on the beach—one was his and the other was God's.

He looked around at all the footprints and noticed that many times there was only one set of footprints. Look over here—only one set of footprints (point). He also noticed that these came during the most troublesome and saddest times of his life.

(Go back and sit down.) This really bothered him, so he asked God about it: "God, you said that once I decided to follow you, you would walk with me all the way. But I see that during the most troublesome times of my life there is only one set of footprints. I don't understand. When I needed you most, why did you leave me?"

And in his dream, God answered: "My precious, precious child, I love you and I would never leave you. During those times of trouble and suffering, when you see only one set of footprints, it was then that I carried you."

Prayer: Dear Father, thank you for loving us and never leaving us. Help us see that our troubles are part of life, and help us grow strong to handle them, with you by our side. Amen.

36

STRAWBERRY EASTER

Do you sometimes think that God must be mad at you because of all the bad things you've done? Sometimes I feel that way. Well, I know a story about this very thing.

Once there were four boys that liked to play together. They had their own fort and they liked to explore and scare girls and get into mischief. Their favorite thing to do was to sneak into old Mr. Thumb's garden and snitch mint leaves to chew on or green tomatoes to throw or even strawberries to eat. Yum! Those were the best.

Old Mr. Thumb didn't like this. Whenever he saw those four boys coming, he would step out on his back porch and watch them. One Fourth of July, the boys got some firecrackers. They knew they were not supposed to light firecrackers, since they were dangerous and could hurt them but they got them anyway. After dark when their families were in their front yards waving sparklers around, the boys met by Mr. Thumb's garden. Do you know what they were going to do? They were going to set those firecrackers off in the garden and watch all the vegetables go splat!

The biggest of the four boys was named Chris. He said, "Hey, wait a minute, you guys. Maybe we'd better not do this."

"Aw, c'mon! Don't be a chicken!" the others said.

"No," said Chris. "I don't think this is right to do to Mr. Thumb.

He really likes this garden." So Chris went off and sat on the side of the hill, watching the other boys.

They took their firecrackers and lit one under a rotten tomato, one under a big zucchini, and finally they lit a firecracker under Mr. Thumb's prize watermelon.

What a mess! The firecrackers went off and blew bits of watermelon, zucchini, and tomato all over the garden. Then they ran as fast as they could.

Now comes the part I was talking about: the next day the four boys felt bad when they looked at the mess in the garden. They were afraid to get anywhere near Mr. Thumb, now. When he drove down the street they hid. They had an awful feeling in their chests, like a black ugly rock.

Finally, Chris said, "I'm going to go make it right. I'll go take the blame."

"No, no!" said the other boys. "You better keep your mouth shut. We haven't been caught yet, have we? And besides, you didn't even do anything."

"Yeah, but look at that mess," said Chris, pointing to the garden. "I'll clean it up and then he won't be mad at us."

The other three boys tried to talk Chris out of it. But Chris walked right up to the old man's door, rang the bell, and volunteered to take the blame. The other boys watched from the bushes across the street. They couldn't believe it. "He must be crazy!" they said.

All that day, Chris worked to clean up Mr. Thumb's garden. They watched Chris sweating, digging, raking, carrying. Once he even cut himself, but he went right on. The boys were beginning to feel bad that Chris was taking all the blame, suffering the punishment himself. They decided to go help Chris in the garden, when old Mr. Thumb walked out the back door towards them.

He called to the three boys. "C'mon over, boys. The work is all done. Let's celebrate with a strawberry!"

The boys looked at each other. Wasn't he mad at them? They were surprised to see the old man smiling!

He smacked his lips over his strawberry, and said, "Yessir, you boys are pretty good kids. I'm proud of you for setting things right," he nodded at all the boys. But inside they still felt guilty. They hadn't helped. Chris had done all the work.

"And," the old man continued, "since you have proven yourselves such fine fellows, you have my permission to enjoy this garden whenever you want. Plenty of strawberries and zucchini and tomatoes for all of us."

They couldn't believe it. They just stared at the old man as he walked back to the house. Chris leaned on his shovel, looking tired and happy. They all began to feel pretty good about the whole thing. Wow, unlimited free strawberries!

Those three boys never forgot what Chris did, taking the blame like that. They thought about it a lot as they grew up. Then, when they were grown, they heard a story about a man named Jesus Christ who went to a cross and died there for their sins. And they recognized it as the same thing, the same story.

37

PIT STOPS
(Memorial Day)

This weekend is a special weekend: Memorial Day weekend. One thing that happens on this weekend is the Indianapolis 500 race. Have any of you seen it on television? The race has already started and the drivers will be going for hours yet.

One interesting thing about this Indy 500 race is the pit stops. A pit stop is when one of the racing cars drives into the pit area and stops. Mechanics change the tires, gas the car up, and fix anything else that might be wrong with the car. There the racecar driver finds out how he is doing in the race—if he is going too slow, who the leaders are, things like that.

Who has seen a pit stop on TV? Those mechanics work fast, don't they? All the workers hurry because they know the pit stop is really important in the race. If a racecar has long pit stops where the mechanics don't do their work well—perhaps they forget to put on one tire and they just mess around—how can that racecar win?

People need pit stops, too. Just like the racecar driver, God's people need to get out of the roaring noisy race of everyday living for a while and stop in with God.

He can tell us how we are doing. He can give us fuel that will keep us going in life. He helps us fix things that may be wrong, like selfishness, or wrong use of our tongues, or something else. And

He refreshes us—just like giving us a brand new set of tires, so we can go zooming back into life again.

How does God do this? I can see at least four ways (hold up one finger at a time):

1. When we pray: God listens to our problems, He answers our prayers and helps us with our troubles.

2. Worship: When we come to church and sing to God, that helps refuel us. We remember and say out loud that God is the biggest, strongest, kindest being there is. Our problems are lifted and we feel better.

3. Read the Bible: The Bible is God's story about God and us. We read it so we can learn who God is. After all, you wouldn't make a pit stop with a stranger, would you? So, we have to know God, and we do that by reading the Bible, and

4. By going to Sunday school. We need to know all we can about God and what other Christian people are like. Our Sunday school teachers help us learn to be good Christians so we can have a good life.

If you see the Indy 500 race on TV, and a pit stop comes up, watch what's going on—the fueling, the new tires, the talking and listening for the driver. And remember, each of us needs pit stops too: 1) prayer, 2) the Bible, 3) worship at church, 4) and Sunday school.

38

BUTTERFLY
(Spring)

I know a girl about your age named Emma. One Sunday in church, her minister said, "I have a surprise for you. Instead of giving my sermon, since it is a lovely spring day outside, I would like each child here to go outside with at least one grownup he *doesn't know,* to find something God made. Bring it back here and together we will look at all the things God made."

Gulp. Emma sat frozen in her place. She didn't want to go outside with some stranger! She took hold of her Grandma's hand and looked up at her, worried. Someone behind them was talking to Grandma. "That will be just fine," Grandma was saying. "You take my granddaughter and I'll take yours. Here, Emma, this is Mr. and Mrs. Stebbins. They will take good care of you."

Before Emma knew what had happened, she was outdoors with Mr. and Mrs. Stebbins, walking across the grass. She didn't know what to say, so she didn't say anything.

"Look at that huge mulberry tree," Mrs. Stebbins said. "All the birds just love those berries. I wish we could take a bird back inside—God certainly made birds—but I don't think we can catch one, do you, Emma?"

Emma shook her head.

"Well now, this tree isn't goin' anywhere," Mr. Stebbins said. "How about taking the tree into church?" She knew he was being silly, and Emma smiled inside herself. She shook her head again. "Maybe a pricker bush?" Mr. Stebbins said. "You want to pick it, Emma, and take it in?"

Emma frowned. "No," she said.

"Probably right. Besides, I'm not sure God made pricker bushes."

Mrs. Stebbins was looking at some tall weeds. "Say, you two, come over here and see what I've found." There were several tall, funny-shaped weeds, like sticks with things on top (hold up milkweed, if available).

"What are those?"

"Just the thing. These, Emma, are milkweed pods. They are the favorite place for certain caterpillars to make cocoons just like this one."

"Cocoons?" Emma looked at the hard, shiny green thing (hold up cocoon, if available). It looked kind of like a nut, stuck to the milkweed.

"Actually, it is a chrysalis," Mrs. Stebbins said. "See, it has a hard skin and there is a butterfly inside."

"There's a butterfly in there?" Emma looked at the small, hard shell. It looked dead and too small to hold a butterfly.

"He's resting now, Emma. And he's changing from a caterpillar to a butterfly. He's growing wings and things."

"Really?" Emma looked carefully at the chrysalis. She knew about caterpillars. They looked like they were made of fuzz. Could a caterpillar grow wings in there?

Carefully, Mr. Stebbins cut the milkweed branch with his pocket knife and they carried it back into the church. Emma was proud when the minister talked about their chrysalis for a long time.

The next Sunday, the chrysalis was still there, right up in the front of the church. "I was watching the chrysalis," the minister said, "and it looks as though it is about ready to open. Maybe we can all see the new butterfly together."

The chrysalis didn't split open during church. Emma went up in front afterwards to see it closer, though, and she noticed a crack in one end. She ran back to tell Mr. Stebbins. He said sure enough, the butterfly was coming out. So they all decided to wait and visit over coffee until the butterfly arrived.

Emma got to sit in the nearly empty church with all the windows open and watch as closely as she wanted. Soon the hard shell was cracked all down one side, and a wet droopy-looking thing hung onto the milkweed branch. Emma didn't dare touch it, but called the others to see. While they watched, the droopy wet thing climbed slowly up the weed, across the altar table, and then stood there, waving its wings. "He's trying to dry out!" Emma said.

"Right," Mr. Stebbins said. "He can't fly until his wings are all dry. Together they watched him wave his wings back and forth, back and forth, then begin to lift off the altar table and flutter down the church aisle.

"Look! He's flying!" said Emma. And as she watched the beautiful black and orange butterfly fly up and over the church pew and out the window.

Emma thought about that butterfly a lot—how good it must feel to be able to wake up from a long sleep and be able to fly all over.

When she was older she heard a song about how we as people are like caterpillars—we walk along the ground every day, eyes close to the earth. Then when we die, it's like going into a cocoon or a chrysalis: it is a quiet and peaceful resting time and we wake up beautiful and able to fly.

39

GOD AND VACATIONS
(Summer)

Vacation time is coming soon. Are any of you going somewhere on vacation—camping or on a trip?

I once knew a little girl named Peggy, and her family liked to go camping. One Sunday in June after Sunday school, when school was almost out, Peggy and her friend Skip were talking about vacations. As they walked out of the church door with their families, Skip waved his arm: "Well, good-bye, God! See you in the fall!"

Peggy was surprised. "Why are you saying good-bye to God, Skip?"

"We're going on vacation. We don't come to church when we're on vacation, so I won't be seeing God."

"But Skip, God isn't only in church. You know that. When you say your prayers at night you must have to say them awfully loud if God has to hear you all the way over at the church!"

"Oh, that's right. I forgot. God is everywhere," Skip said.

"Right, and He goes on vacation with us in our family," Peggy said.

"He does? How can God go on vacation with you?"

"Right before we leave, we all stand at the door and hold hands and talk to God. We invite Him to come with us and ask Him to protect us and help us have a good trip. Once we forgot, though. . . ."

"Yeah? What happened?"

"Well, the car engine started making a funny noise and Mom left the lunch at home in the refrigerator and everyone was crabby. It was awful."

"What did you do?" Skip asked her.

"We thought about going back home and starting over, but it was too far. So, we just stopped the car and held hands and prayed right there. Then everything went better."

"Do you go to church when you are on vacation?" Skip asked Peggy.

"Sure, sometimes in different towns. It's interesting. There are big churches, small churches; we even went to a drive-in church once."

"A drive-in church?"

"Yes, or sometimes we have prayers at night in the camper. It's easy, 'cause you are all right there together."

"So, God goes on vacation with you, hey?" Skip said.

"Yup."

"Do you think He would go with our family?"

"If you asked Him, sure. God is everywhere."

Prayer: Dear Father, watch over us as we travel this summer. Protect us on the highway, keep us from squabbling when we get tired and hot, and bless this special time we have together. Thank you for vacations. Amen.

40

NEW BOY AT SCHOOL (Autumn)

Eddie had just moved into a new neighborhood. The first day of school was coming and Eddie was going to have to go to a new school.

Have any of you ever moved? Have you ever had to go to a new school?

Then you know how Eddie felt. He was worried. He didn't know anybody in his new neighborhood yet, and here he was going to have to ride on a noisy school bus to a school full of people he didn't know. The whole thing was kind of scary. Eddie wished he was back in his old neighborhood with all his old friends and his old school, where he knew his way around.

The first day of school was getting closer and closer. Sometimes Eddie would stand at the window and look outside at the new neighborhood, just worrying about what school was going to be like.

Eddie's mother knew how he felt. One day she sat down by the window next to him and said, "Eddie, I have an idea that may help you on the first day of school."

"Good," said Eddie, hoping she would say something like quit school or stay home and be sick or move back to the old house.

"No, you are going to have to face this new thing, Eddie," she said. "But I know one secret that will help: get your mind off yourself and how scared you are, and spend all your time and energy helping someone else," Eddie's mother smiled.

Boy, thought Eddie, *what a dumb idea.* Here he had enough problems of his own and she was suggesting he solve someone else's, too! Sometimes Eddie thought grownups just didn't make sense.

Later that day, Eddie was riding around the street on his bike, and he saw a boy about five years old playing with some other kids on their driveway. The five-year-old called to him, "Hey, what's your name? I'm Mark! Did you just move into that house?"

Eddie nodded and he stayed by the curb awhile, watching the kids ride their tricycles and make chalk drawings on the driveway. Eddie was older than these kids. It was kind of fun to watch them.

The next morning was the awful day: first day of school. Eddie stood out by the curb like a nail in the grass, all stiff and straight. His stomach was fluttering. He stepped onto the bus like a tin soldier.

It was noisy inside, just like his old bus. Uh, oh, Edddie saw who the bully was going to be already—that big kid doing all the yelling.

But what was this? Coming down the aisle was Mark, the five-year-old from down the street. He must be starting kindergarten. *Boy, look at him,* Eddie thought, *he looks scared to death. His face is all white and his eyes are all big and he looks like he's trying not to cry.*

Eddie suddenly moved over on his bus seat and said, "Hey, Mark, here's a seat. Come sit with me." Mark looked up at Eddie and then the bus jerked ahead and Mark nearly fell. Eddie grabbed him just in time and sat him down. "You hafta find a seat and sit down before the bus moves, Mark. Or else hang onto one of the seats. Otherwise you fall down." Eddie explained this, but Mark didn't say a word.

"Hey, what's that you have pinned on your jacket, Mark? Your name, and our street, and what's this number 326?"

Mark looked at Eddie, stricken, and shook his head.

"You don't know? Well, Mark, maybe it's the room you are supposed to go to in school."

Mark thought a minute and nodded. But he still looked almost paralyzed. *Boy,* thought Eddie, *and here I thought I was worried!*

"Hey, Mark. Tell ya what. I'll take you to your room 326 on the way to my room, okay? We can find our new rooms together."

Mark looked really relieved and nodded. Then, Mark reached his little hand next to Eddie and hung onto the corner of Eddie's jacket. Eddie felt all warm and strong. He'd take care of this scared little kid.

From that day on they were buddies. Eddie was surprised at how the new school wasn't as bad as he thought. And his new neighborhood was pretty nice, too.

In a little while Mark was brave enough to walk to his room by himself. Soon Mark made friends with other kindergarteners on the bus and sat with them. But, by this time Eddie had also made friends. They thought he was a nice kid because of the way he took care of Mark.

In fact, everything turned out pretty well and finally Eddie realized that what his mom said was right: when you are in trouble, reach out and help someone else. It gets your mind off your own worries and makes everyone a lot happier.

Prayer: Dear God, help us remember that it is in giving that we receive. Amen.

SUBJECT INDEX

Building Our Faith
1, 5, 9, 10, 13, 14, 19, 37, 39

Death
2, 5, 18, 29, 38

Divorce
33

Family Life
4, 7, 8, 11, 15, 22, 31, 34, 39

Fears
5, 21, 26, 29, 40

Forgiveness
4, 15, 36

God's Authority
11, 14, 27

God's Love for Us
5, 13, 28, 30

God's Power
1, 13, 17, 23, 39

The Holy Spirit
1, 5, 21, 32

Jesus
10, 25, 36

Justification
36

Life's Mysteries
2, 6, 12, 13, 14, 18, 36

Love One Another
1, 3, 4, 6, 10, 15, 22, 28, 34, 40

Man's Will vs. God's Plan
(Willfulness)
2, 3, 9, 11, 13, 14, 20, 27

Materialism
16, 23, 31

New Situations
16, 19, 32, 39, 40

Responsibility
7, 8, 11

Troubles
5, 6, 12, 16, 17, 23, 35